D0330485

The Anatomy of Anti-Semitism
and Other Essays on
Religion and Race

The Anatomy of Anti-Semitism and Other Essays on Religion and Race

JAMES DAANE

ASSISTANT EDITOR
CHRISTIANITY TODAY

WM. B. EERDMANS PUBLISHING COMPANY
GRAND RAPIDS, MICHIGAN

TABOR COLLEGE
LIBRARY
HILLSBORO, KANSAS

35163

JUL 5 '66

Copyright © 1965 by Wm. B. Eerdmans Publishing Co.
All rights reserved
Library of Congress Catalog Card Number: 65-18090
Printed in the United States of America

PHOTOLITHOPRINTED BY GRAND RAPIDS BOOK MANUFACTURERS, INC.
GRAND RAPIDS, MICHIGAN
1965

Preface

WITHOUT THE PRODDING ENCOURAGEMENT OF OTHERS
this collection of essays on religion, race, and morals
would not have appeared. Every essay in this volume,
except the one on the New Morality, was written for
one-shot appearances in either *Christianity Today* or
The Reformed Journal.

On first seeing their babies, mothers often experience
an instinctive impulse to reject them. I experience the
same feeling, not indeed toward babies, but toward anything I have wirtten. There is one difference — in my
case the feeling persists. It was, therefore, impossible
to republish these essays without extensive revision. In
the process, they have also been updated. Whether the
additional time and effort expended have made them
better or worse is not for me to decide. I only know
that the added travail was pleasant and that the revision
has been so extensive that my requests for permission to
reprint them were more an exercise of politeness than
of duty.

Written at scattered times and places, these essays nonetheless turn on the hinge of a single theme. This was no conscious achievement. Their unplanned unity stems from the fact that any person's mind fastens on selected facets of religion and life, partly because no one's mind is large enough to wrap itself around them all.

The problem of race in our time is only on the most superficial level a problem of color or nationality. Whenever racism is defended, it is not done on the basis of color or national origin. When a white rejects a Negro "because he is black," or a Gentile rejects a Jew "because of his nationality," color and nationality really have little to do with it. Racism is rather defended by an appeal to undesirable traits that allegedly attach to color or national origin. The superficiality of this is betrayed, however, whenever a colored man or a Jew who does not possess these traits is nonetheless rejected by the blanket rejection on his race, or nationality. The basic motivations of rejection are largely unconscious. This accounts for the meager results that sociological, physiological, and psychological research and studies have had in the elimination of racial prejudice on the level where it is actually practiced.

In this exercise of racial prejudice a man stands godlike astride humanity and selects himself and some of his fellows. What is this but a proud assertion that one is — together with those one chooses — the elect, the favored of God? Racial prejudice is a secular version of divine election — a sinful human usurpation of prerogatives that belong to God alone. As Pharisaism was a perversion of divine election and a distinctively religious phenomenon, so racism finds its sharpest expression in Christian societies, and it is here frequently defended by ap-

6

peal to biblical teaching. How often Christians have made the exegetically untenable appeal to the divine curse on the sons of Ham to proffer biblical proof that the Negro is under a curse of God! And the Apostle Paul felt the necessity of warning Gentiles against that sin of pride which construed their own election as a proof of the divine rejection of the Jews.

It is, furthermore, remarkable that many people who make no Christian profession are offended at a God who elects and rejects men, yet they regard it as their unquestionable right to accept some men and to reject others with a majestic brush of their hand. Because of its belief in election, Calvinism has long been castigated by people who themselves arbitrarily reject vast numbers of people, not on account of their sin, but merely on the basis of skin color or national origin, factors for which Christian truth holds no man responsible. What such people, on moral ground, deny God the right to do, they themselves do on grounds that are amoral.

Racism is at bottom a religious phenomenon. When viewed from the Christian perspective, racism (whether grounded on color or national origin) is seen in the light of God's election of the Jew — rather than the Gentile, whether colored or white — and ultimately in the light of God's election of Jesus, the Jew, as the Christ in whom alone men of every race and color can find their unity.

The ultimate solution to the problem of racism does not lie in the consideration that all men are equal because all are created by God. Racism is a phenomenon of a fallen humanity. Its solution, therefore, lies in the recognition that the right to accept or reject any man lies with God alone, with Him who sovereignly exercised this right and chose a Jew, Jesus of Nazareth, to be the Christ.

It is only within an acknowledgment that Jesus is God's Elect that men of all races and national origins will find their unity, and the grace to accept each other fully.

God's election of man is the answer to man's rejection of man — which is the essence of racism.

Whatever can and must be said about the Jews' *religious* misinterpretation of their own election, neither the people of the Old or New Testament knew anything of a racial prejudice based on color or mere nationality.

It is the contention of this writer that even the Christian Church has broached the problem of racism too exclusively in sociological and ethnic terms and too little from the biblical, religious perspective. Even when it has been done from the latter perspective, it has been done too exclusively in terms of the implications of creation, and almost not at all in terms of God's election of the Jews, the Gentiles, and particularly of Jesus Christ. If these essays widen the crack on the biblical perspective, they will serve a large purpose.

— JAMES DAANE
Arlington, Virginia

Contents

PREFACE   5

1   THE ANATOMY OF ANTI-SEMITISM   13

2   CHRISTIAN, JEW, AND NEGRO   37

3   AT THE CROSS   55

4   THE GLORY OF GOD   62

5   THE NEW MORALITY   69

The Anatomy of Anti-Semitism and Other Essays on Religion and Race

1

The Anatomy of Anti-Semitism

IT IS A TENET OF CHRISTIANITY THAT HISTORY MUST BE interpreted theologically. The inner meaning of history does not lie in the dialectical movements of economic materialism, as Marx contended, nor does it lie in a biological evolutionary process, nor in the spiritual struggle of the human spirit for freedom. The key that unlocks the meaning of history is none of these. It is Jesus Christ, and more specifically, Jesus Christ crucified.

Although Christians vary in their formulations as to precisely what occurred at the Cross, they are in agreement that the Cross was an event of reconciliation. Here God and man are reconciled, and within this reconciliation man is reconciled to man. A profound and classic aspect of this reconciliation is the reconciliation of Jew and Gentile. Indeed, it is biblical teaching that this reconciliation of Jew and Gentile in the unity of the Church is the sign to the world of God's eternal purpose to sum up all things in Christ.

From ancient times the Jews, according to biblical teaching, were elected by God to be his chosen people. The Old Testament is the history of this elect nation,

13

and during the time of this history the Gentiles lay out-side God's elective action. St. Paul declares that the Gentiles were "at that time" without God and without hope in the world. But this cleavage between Jew and Gentile, introduced by God's election of the Jews, has now been healed through the Cross. By the death of Christ, Paul informs the Ephesians, the "wall of par-tition" between Jews and Gentiles has been broken down. Through the Cross, Christ has removed the enmity, reconciled Jew and Gentile, and of the two made "one new man, so making peace." Unity has been achieved through the reconciling effect of the Cross, and the Gentiles are now no longer "aliens of the commonwealth of Israel," no longer "strangers and foreigners, but fellow citizens with the saints, and of the household of God."

Thus the deepest cleavage between men is not that between Negro and white, democratic and totalitarian societies, East and West, or civilized and uncivilized peoples, but the cleavage posited by God's election be-tween Jew and Gentile. This deepest of all divisions be-tween men was, according to both the Old and New Tes-taments, introduced by God. Sin has wrought many dis-unities between men. This deepest division, however, is not effected by man's sins, but by God's gracious elec-tion. It was God's election that posited the "wall of partition" between Jew and Gentile; this wall therefore was higher than any Berlin wall, any bamboo or iron curtain. Moreover, the measure of the enmity, the depth of the antithesis between Jew and Gentile, cor-responded to the dimension of the division wrought by the divine election of the Jews.

Nonetheless, this enmity is no ground for anti-Semitism today, for the Cross according to the Christian's New

Testament annulled the enmity and made peace between Jew and Gentile. And, to round out the sketch of this aspect of a Christian theological understanding of history, the Jews are still, according to Paul, God's chosen people. The thought that they are not elicited Paul's vigorous statement, "God forbid." This for Paul is unthinkable because the "gifts and calling of God are not repented of." God's election does not change. This chosen people will in some future day, Paul asserts, turn to the crucified Christ, and this turning will have tremendous repercussions for good upon the history of the whole world.

YET, IN SPITE OF THIS BIBLICAL TEACHING, ANTI-Semitism remains to this very day. The tragic experience of the Jews during the days of Hitlerian Germany stands as a towering landmark to the dimensions of its depth and horror. There is nothing in the history of mankind that approximates that hatred of Gentile for Jew seen in the methodical attempt of the Nazis to destroy the whole Jewish nation.

Serious attempts are now being made by Protestantism and Roman Catholicism to alleviate anti-Semitic prejudice. The conscience of the Christian Church has been stricken by the incredible sufferings imposed on the Jews in the Second World War. Apparently nothing less was capable of smiting the Christian conscience into an examination of its own contribution to anti-Semitism. Both Roman Catholicism and Protestantism are examining their catechetical and Sunday-school lessons to discover material that needlessly promotes anti-Jewish prejudice. In recent years the *pro perfidis judaeis* in the Roman Good Friday prayer for the Jews was given the milder translation of "unfaithful"

15

and "unbelieving." In 1955 the custom of kneeling in the Good Friday prayers for the Jews was reinstated — after almost 1200 years! Progress is being made. Surely there is no place in Christian prayer and worship of God to press before the Almighty the sinfulness of the Jews in crucifying Christ.

Yet the very attempt to uncover and eradicate the roots of anti-Semitism tends both to reveal and to deepen prejudice and tensions, and it does so to the extent that the roots are sought in religion. Analysis of anti-Semitism tends to create what the analysis seeks to eradicate, as does, for example, the ecumenical study of the causes of denominationalism. Yet the probing must go on. For Jules Isaac is right in his contention that anti-Semitism has religious rather than secular or pagan roots and that its deepest roots are in Christian soil.

Isaac declares that all through his studies of this problem he has seen "Christian anti-Semitism as the powerful trunk, with deep and multiple roots, upon which have been grafted other varieties of anti-Semitism, even varieties as anti-Christian as Nazi racialism" (*Has Anti-Semitism Roots in Christianity?,* pp. 55, 56). The last part of this quotation shows that the attempts to put out the fires of anti-Semitism tend to stoke up the fire. "Historical research," says Isaac, "reveals that Christian anti-Semitism is much worse than its pagan predecessor: worse by its content — which is essentially theological" (p. 55). In his book *The Teaching of Contempt: Christian Roots of Anti-Semitism,* he asserts that "anti-Semitism is profoundly rooted in Christianity" (p. 23) and that "it may be affirmed with complete confidence that the vast majority of Christians — or those recognized as such — are anti-Semites" (p. 24). "Yes, even after Auschwitz, Maidenek, Dubno, and

16

Treblinka, Christian anti-Semitism is still alive. It does not perceive, it does not wish to perceive the hidden bond linking it with Nazi anti-Semitism . . . " (pp. 25, 26). And for all his restraint and considerable degree of objectivity, he declares that "it is impossible to forget, because it is an essential factor, that Hitlerian racialism appeared on ground which previous centuries before had prepared for it. Did the Nazis spring from nothing or from the bosom of a Christian people?" Such remarks from a competent historian and a man of sober restraint indicate how difficult it is to avoid stoking the anti-Semitic fire at the very time one is attempting to put it out.

Yet this probing attempt to discover the roots of anti-Semitism must go on, for Isaac is correct in finding the roots of anti-Semitism to be religious, and more specifically "Christian," that is, that they are sunk and nourished in Christian soil. It cannot be denied that the Nazi attempt to exterminate the Jewish people occurred in Germany, which might be called the modern cradle of Christianity in the Western world. Indeed, it may be asserted that the only anti-Semitism that is of any considerable significance and concern arises within a Christian context. (This is not to deny that there is also a considerable degree of Jewish feeling against Christians for specifically Christian reasons that Christians cannot repudiate without repudiating their Christianity. For varied and obvious reasons this has played no great role in history, yet the fact that it has no name [as has anti-Semitism] does not mean that it does not exist.)

Isaac asserts that the first expressions of anti-Semitism arose in pre-Christian times. When the Jews in the Diaspora, though existing among pagan peoples, remained true to their Jewish religious beliefs they prac-

17

ticed a kind of separatism and experienced a kind of anti-Semitism. Isaac asks Christians to remember that this separatism was by divine command, and Jews were obliged to practice it. He quotes Leviticus 20:26, where God says to the Jews, "I have separated you from the people, that you should be mine." Israel was chosen by God to be his peculiar possession. Isaac has a right to ask Christians to remember and honor Israel's election — something that Christians frequently do not do and their unwillingness to do so is itself a form of anti-Semitism. The Church may never ignore Israel's election.

The chief cause of Christian anti-Semitism, according to Isaac, is the accusation of Christians that the Jews are guilty of deicide, that is, by their crucifixion of Jesus Christ they killed [the Son of] God. In his *Teaching of Contempt,* Isaac asserts that "no idea has been more destructive and has had more deadly effect on the scattered Jewish minorities living in Christian countries than the pernicious view of them as the 'deicide people' " (p. 109). But with this we are back at the Cross, back to the place where, according to the New Testament teaching and Christian confession, the wall of enmity was broken down, the place where God made peace and of Jew and Gentile made one new man.

Thus both Isaac's analysis of anti-Semitism from the Jewish viewpoint, and the Christian analysis of the dissolution of anti-Semitism, bring us back to the Cross. It is not surprising, therefore, that the Cross is of special concern in Jewish-Christian relations.

The question of responsibility for the crucifixion of Jesus Christ continues to be an irritant in Jewish-Christian relations. A preliminary report of a continuing five-year study of anti-Semitism in the United States has recently been issued by the Anti-Defamation League of B'nai B'rith. The report, based on questionnaires sent adult members of Protestant churches, shows that 69 percent of those questioned believe that the Jews are the group "most responsible" for the death of Christ, and that this view is more extensively held in conservative, fundamentalist churches than in liberal churches. Benjamin R. Epstein, national director of the Anti-Defamation League, reported that this view continues to be a "cruel, critical factor in perpetuating anti-Semitic prejudice." He declared that the report's preliminary findings "merely reinforce us in our long-time speculation on the role of church institutions in developing ambivalent and often tragic attitudes toward Jews — a speculation that led to the study itself." And he added that the treatment given Jews by Christians represents a "failure" of Christendom.

How should the Christian churches meet this charge of failure? Can they dismiss the charge by asserting that the study was prejudiced to prove the "speculation" that initiated it? Can they appeal to the historical records of the New Testament and prove that the Jews are in fact "most responsible?" Anti-Semitism is no inexplicable mystery. There is an answer to it, and the Church owes it to herself as much as to the Jews to make this answer clear.

THERE ARE TWO ASPECTS OF THE PROBLEM OF THE crucifixion of Jesus Christ. One is the historical: what actually happened? The other aspect is the theological: what is the theological interpretation of this event and of the complex of events that led to it? Jules Isaac is right when he asserts that any decent theology must go beyond history; and he is equally right when he con-

TABOR COLLEGE LIBRARY HILLSBORO, KANSAS

35163

tends that a theological interpretation of history may not violate the facts of history. But, while the Christian Church cannot assume that the Jews will accept the theological interpretation given to the history of Christ's death in the New Testament, it has as much right to ask the Jews to honor the Christian's acceptance of the New Testament writings as Isaac has a right to ask Christians to recognize and understand that the Old Testament enjoined a separated existence upon Jews.

Isaac himself, however, is not willing to honor the Church's respect for her New Testament writings. He insists that the New Testament Gospel writers distorted the story of the crucifixion by placing the major blame upon the Jews and a minimum blame upon the Romans who, according to Isaac, were in fact chiefly responsible for Jesus' death. Jules Isaac's contention that the Romans were responsible and not the Jews is widely held among Jewish people. Why did the early Christians blame the Jews? Because, says Isaac, they feared Rome and her reprisals and hence blamed the Jews, who were quite helpless. This is a strange reconstruction, particularly when we consider that the first persecution of the Christians was done, as Isaac admits, by Jews; and that the early Christians were frequently imprisoned by Jews. Isaac's reconstruction is especially unconvincing if it is true, as he urges, that the Sanhedrin were collaborators with the Roman government and that they were the group that desired the death of Jesus. But the weakest point in Isaac's case against the New Testament record is that the placing of the blame upon the Romans leaves the crucifixion of Christ *without adequate motivation.* Why would the Romans want to crucify Christ? The question is especially pertinent in the light of Isaac's contention that Jesus hid his messianic claim, a claim

20

that would be disturbing to Rome, which wanted not Jewish messiahs but peace. It is obvious that no explanation of the death of Christ can be regarded as adequate that lacks a motive for the killing.

According to the New Testament records, Jews desired, plotted, and promoted the execution of Jesus (Matthew 27:1). No rewriting of history by those interested in freeing the Jews from responsibility for the crucifixion, or by script writers of modern movies, dispels these claims of the New Testament historical records. The records reveal, moreover, that it was not the "common people," nor the "publicans and sinners," nor the Jewish drunkard or woman of the street who demanded the death of Christ. Not a lunatic fringe, nor a religious extreme right or left, nor the denizens of an ancient skid row brought about the execution of Christ. It was rather the Jewish religious leadership — the scribes and Pharisees, the priests, men of the holy place — that took council together to put Jesus to death. It was the chief priests and elders who moved among the rabble on the night of Jesus' trial, inciting them to cry, "Crucify him" (Matthew 27:30). It was the Jewish religious hierarchy that pressured Pilate and brought false witnesses into court to testify against Jesus (Matthew 27:29; Mark 14:55, 56). All this is not a fabric of prejudice against the Jews but the claims of the historical record of the New Testament.

According to the same historical records, Jesus was *betrayed* to his death. Now no one is ever betrayed by his enemies; one can be betrayed only by a friend, for a betrayal is by definition a turning of friendship against a friend. Jesus was a Jew; his friends were Jewish. He was delivered into the hands of the enemy by one who sat at his table and ate with him (John 13:18). And eating together, then even more than now, was an exercise of friendship. A betrayal has to be an "inside job"; a betrayer must be one called "friend," one from whom a kiss is customary. The New Testament record repeatedly stresses that Jesus was betrayed by "one of the twelve" (Matthew 26:14; Mark 14:20). It was to "his own" (John 1:11) that Jesus came, and it was "his own" who received him not.

These historical data relate the relevant facts of the Jewish role in the crucifixion of Christ. If the destruction of another carries responsibility, then Jewish responsibility is a matter of historical fact. Even from the Jewish point of view, a man was destroyed; and it is better to face the fact of history than weakly to suggest, as the Anti-Defamation League study does, that the similarity between the words "Judas" and "Judaism" tends to perpetuate anti-Semitism. Judas was a Jew, and a people as conscious of their unity as the Jews are cannot dismiss him, nor hope to play convincingly with the accident of his name.

Some Jewish writers assert that a few "renegade" Jews participated in the crucifixion of Christ, but seem appalled at the idea that the whole Jewish people shared in their guilt. But does not the Jewish Old Testament teach a solidarity of the Jewish people in the good as well as in the evil? Is it not true that the history of the Old Testament Israel is the history of her kings. Could not one say that as "the kings fared, so fared the people"? Surely Israel's election bespeaks solidarity. And the very idea of solidarity implies a mutual involvement in blessing as well as in responsibility. Where solidarity obtains, you cannot have the one without the other.

BEFORE THE QUESTION MAY BE RAISED AS TO THE *theological* interpretation that the New Testament places on these facts, the Gentile Christian Church must also face the historical facts of the Gentile role and responsibility for the crucifixion of Jesus.

According to the New Testament, Jesus identified himself as the "Son of man," and referred to the prophetic prediction that the Son of man "shall be delivered unto the Gentiles, and shall be mocked, and shamefully treated, and spit upon: and they shall scourge him and put him to death. . ." (Luke 18:32, 33). If Jews tend to ignore their historical role, honesty compels the admission that few Christian preachers preach on this text. The same records assert that he was tried in a Roman court — the highest structured justice in the Gentile world of the time — and was crowned with thorns by Romans and condemned under Pontius Pilate, a Roman judge. He died at the hands of Roman soldiers, in the Roman manner, on a cross. And the Romans were Gentiles! Although Pilate was reluctant and his wife uneasy, no Gentile rose to protest the injustice of Christ's condemnation. The reality of Pilate's responsibility and its *creedal* significance were recognized by the early Church when it recorded in the Apostles' Creed that Jesus "suffered under Pontius Pilate." By Jewish insistence *and* by Gentile instrumentality, Christ was crucified. Jewish insistence alone was impotent, having no authority to put a man to death. Roman power alone was also impotent, being reluctant and without motivation to complete the betrayal of one who was not a Roman Messiah and hid his messianic claims from the Gentiles. Together Jew and Gentile accomplished the deed. Neither, therefore, is without guilt.

But is one group more guilty than the other? Are

the Jews "most responsible?" This is a crucial question in Jewish-Christian relationships. It is interesting to observe that the preliminary report of the Anti-Defamation League shows it was the membership of the liberal rather than of the conservative, fundamentalist churches that most frequently gave the right answer, i.e., that the Jews are not "most responsible." But the question of the greater responsibility and guilt is crucial only within anti-Semitism, *for the question itself is the basic source of religious anti-Semitism.* There would be none of that anti-Semitism which concerns the Anti-Defamation League study if the question were not asked at all — by anyone. And it ought not to be asked, because the question is illegitimate.

Nowhere in the New Testament are the Jews said to be condemned and rejected by God for their role in the crucifixion of Jesus Christ. Nor are they anywhere in the New Testament condemned and rejected by the primitive New Testament Church. Their role is indeed not denied, but the Jews are not therefore presented as a people rejected by God and therefore a people to be rejected by men. This cannot be too strongly emphasized, for here lies the deepest root of Christian anti-Semitism. This simple fact, that the Jews are not rejected by God for their part in crucifying Christ, has been widely ignored by the Christian Church. There has been all too much in Christian thought, practice, and teaching to give point to the comment of Jules Isaac: "Now many Jewish children have heard a small Christian companion say: 'I won't play with you, you killed Jesus Christ'" (*Has Anti-Semitism Roots in Christianity?,* p. 66).

It is Christ on the Cross, not the Jews, who is rejected and accursed by God. On the Cross, Christ prayed also for the Jews: "Father, forgive them for they know not

24

what they do." The primitive New Testament Church did not reject the Jews but, on the contrary, preached the gospel to them. On Pentecost the gospel was preached to Jews only. Paul speaking "in Christ," that is, speaking precisely as a Christian, declares that he could wish himself accursed from Christ for the sake of "his brethren according to the flesh." Paul also declares that the Gospel is "the power of God unto salvation to everyone that believeth" and it is this not only for the Jew, but for the "Jew first." Throughout his Roman epistle Paul urges this priority of the Jew. He was unable to define the gospel apart from the Jew and his priority. Indeed, only with considerable difficulty did the early Christian Jewish Church learn that the gospel is also for the Gentiles. It was only *after* the general rejection of the gospel by the Jews that Paul turned to the Gentiles. The assumption that the Jews are rejected for crucifying Christ can only be held against the clear teaching and the plain facts of the New Testament record. The Jew, like the Gentile, is only rejected by God and brought under judgment after he has rejected the crucified and living Christ as the Christ confronts them in the preaching of the gospel. An anti-Semitism grounded in Jewish responsibility for the Cross disqualifies the Christian Church both for understanding and for preaching the gospel.

The question whether the Jews are "most responsible" for the crucifixion is therefore an illegitimate question. But after the recent destruction of six million Jews, one million eight hundred thousand of whom were children, no Christian has a right to score the Jews for seeking to unearth the cause of anti-Semitism by raising the question of who is "most responsibile." Anti-Semitism is a specifically Christian sin. While the question ideally ought not be raised by either Jew or Gentile, the Gentile

Christian is in no position to criticize the Jew for raising it. Least of all is the Christian in the moral position to answer the question in the affirmative. Since the Gentile is also responsible for the death of Christ, as the New Testament plainly shows, he is in no moral position to blame the Jew, and least of all is he in a moral position to charge him with greater culpability. He who shares guilt with another for a sinful act has no moral warrant for condemning the other — not even if it can be objectively established that the other's guilt is greater.

Here lies the spiritual solvent that ought to dissolve anti-Semitism within the Christian community. Penitent for his own role in crucifying the Son of God, cognizant of his infinite guilt for such an act, the Gentile Christian can, within the spirit of true repentance, condemn only himself. When he thinks of the sins of other sinners — which he naturally does and must do — if he is truly sorry for his own sins, he can only compare other sinners *favorably* with himself. With Paul, he can only say about sinners: "of whom I am chief." Confession of one's own responsibility for the death of Christ involves the recognition that one's guilt is infinite. Where this is recognized and acknowledged, how can the sin of another be regarded as *greater?* How can the Jew be regarded as "most" responsible?

When this essay first appeared in the pages of *Christianity Today,* I received a number of letters reminding me of that statement of Jesus to Pilate in which he says that the Jews were more guilty than he. My respondents felt that this cinched the argument of greater Jewish responsibility. Yet, significantly, none of them indicated any desire to make anything of their point for the establishment of greater Jewish guilt.

We are here confronted with an aspect of authentic

Christian spirituality that all Christians intuitively sense but few seem able to understand in terms of conscious reflection. There are judgments that Christ may make, that God may pronounce, but that Christians may not make. Jesus may urge that the Jews have greater guilt for his death than Pilate. But may Pilate? If Pilate would utter the same words, he would be saying something altogether different. Again, Paul says that he is the chief of sinners. Was Paul telling the truth? He was neither lying nor exaggerating. Nonetheless, it would not be truth if you or I said this about Paul. Suppose a minister made the special point in a sermon that Paul was indeed the worst of all sinners. Wouldn't his congregation intuitively sense that there was something essentially unchristian about such a sermon?

Through the knowledge of his faith, the Christian knows what he did when he nailed Christ to the Cross. With this knowledge he can only say with Paul that had the Jews known what they were doing, "they would not have crucified the Lord of glory" (I Corinthians 2: 8). With the knowledge of his own sin, the Christian cannot impute the "most responsibility" to the Jews without denying the genuineness of his own confession. By casting stones at the Jews for the death of Christ, the Gentile Christian reveals the spirit of New Testament Pharisaism, the spirit that desired, plotted, and promoted the crucifixion of Jesus Christ.

There is no place in Christian prayer or attitude for the *perfidi Judaei*. For this is to urge the guilt of the Jew for the crucifixion even before God. Peter in his Pentecostal sermon recognizes the guilt of the Jews and declares that they took Christ and with wicked hands slew him, but Peter is not condemning the Jews (he was one himself). He is preaching the gospel to

27

them that they might be saved. Similarly in Acts 4 the early Christians under Jewish persecution mentioned in their prayers that God's annointed was crucified by Jews and Gentiles, but they did not do this in the spirit of judgment and condemnation. On the contrary, under this persecution, which they viewed as an extension of that which sent Christ to the Cross, they prayed for special boldness to preach the Word of God to the Jews for their salvation.

The Church may never charge the Jews with the "greater responsibility" for the death of Christ; nor may it ignore the plain New Testament teaching that the Jews are not rejected by God for the crucifixion. If rejected at all, they are rejected for their rejection of the Christ of the gospel.

THERE IS ANOTHER SOURCE OF ANTI-SEMITISM FOUND within the Christian Church, related to but not identical with that which appeals to the Jewish crucifixion of Christ. Paul in his epistle to the Romans teaches that a judgment of God has befallen Israel for its rejection of the gospel. This judgment is in part, and for a time only. It does not mean that God has cast off his people (Romans 11:1). Paul rejects this idea with a "God forbid." God has not cast off his people whom he foreknew (Romans 11:2). The persistence of a remnant is proof (Romans 11:2-5). And Paul clinches his argument that Israel is not a divine "castaway" when he says that "the gifts and the calling of God are not repented of" (Romans 11:29). Israel's sin cannot undo her election; having chosen Israel, God does not change his mind. His election shall stand.

The Church, however, has often misunderstood this temporary judgment of God upon Israel in the way that

Paul, prior to becoming a Christian on the Damascus road, misunderstood the Cross. Paul knew the teaching of the book of Deuteronomy (as the book of Galatians indicates) which asserts, "He that is hanged is accursed of God" (21:23). From the fact that God in his providence allowed Christ to hang on the tree of the Cross, Paul deduced that Christ was accursed and rejected of God. And Paul felt that if God rejected him, he should do the same. He accordingly thought he was doing God a service when he persecuted the Christian Church and sought the imprisonment of those who preached Christ for acceptance by others. As a Christian, Paul understood the error of this view. Once Paul learned that the Christ, whom he thought rejected of God because of the Cross, was in fact accepted by God and exalted in the highest glory at God's right hand, he completely changed his mind about the Cross and became willing to be himself accursed for his Jewish brethren (Romans 9:1-3 and 10:1). Looking back on his error, Paul could say that he sinned in ignorance.

The Church, however, against the plain teaching of Romans, has often taken the position that while an occasional Jew is saved, the Jewish nation as a whole is no longer God's elect nation and, having been forever cast off by God, it has no religious future. It has often been argued that this final rejection of the elect people has accrued because the Jews as a whole rejected the Christ of gospel proclamation. The Church has often felt — in the manner of Paul prior to his conversion — that it could adopt much the same attitude toward the Jewish people as it thought God to have adopted. Thus Dom Gueranger could write in 1841, "The spectacle of an entire people placed under a curse for having crucified the Son of God gives Christian food for thought. . . . This immense atonement for an infinite crime must continue until the end of the world." And Father Ferdinand Prat in *Jesus-Christ* declared, "The vengeance of God will fall without mercy on this deicide people." In both these assertions the Jews are forever cursed, and cursed for the crucifixion. For this there is not the slightest biblical support. Father Fessard in *Pax nostra* wrote of "the murderous people eternally nailed to the crossroads where the destinies of mankind meet and intersect" (quoted by Jules Isaac). Christians have often thought that God rejected the Jews, and that they were justified in doing the same; and they too often practiced and justified anti-Semitism on this ground.

Christians are not God. God may curse; they may not. God may damn; they may only bless, and curse not. Vengeance, judgment, and rejection belong to God alone. A pre-Christian Paul persecuted the Christian Church on the fallacious assumption that what God did he could also do. God alone may punish the Jews for their rejection of the crucified and resurrected Christ; the Church may not. God may punish his enemies; the Church may only love its enemies and pray for them.

MOREOVER, IF THE JEWS REJECTED HIM WHO IS *par excellence* God's elect, Jesus Christ, the Church in the practice of anti-Semitism rejects the nation of God's election, and in doing so rejects the gospel, which in its very nature is "for the Jew first." According to the Bible, the Jews are enemies of the gospel, but, as Paul says to the Gentiles, "for your sakes" (Romans 11:28). In the inscrutable wisdom of God, whose ways are past finding out, the Gentiles have entered into salvation through the Jewish rejection of it. In Ephesians, Paul

30

admonishes Gentile Christians: "Wherefore remember . . . that ye were at that time separate from Christ, alienated from the commonwealth of Israel, and strangers from the covenants of promise, having no hope and without God in the world" (Ephesians 2:11, 12). The Gentiles, according to Paul, have entered into the covenant and the inheritance of the Jews, into *their* salvation and glory. "Salvation is of the Jews" (John 4:22b), and Gentiles are saved through the Jews' Messiah. Christ was a Jew. In coming to the Jews, he came to "his own." He is Israel's glory.

How did Gentiles, who were "aliens" and "strangers," become "fellow citizens" and "members of the household of faith" (Ephesians 2:19)? How did the outsider become an insider? This historical transition is one of the basic themes running through the epistle of Paul to the Romans. The transition was a historical event. It is therefore real and to be taken seriously. What is revealed is not a timeless, eternal truth but rather one that became real in the historical happening. The historical movement in which this truth becomes truth and is revealed as truth is not simple and direct; it is an uneven movement, a historical zigzag. The truth thus revealed is not simple and immediate, but one that calls for a deep and sensitive spiritual comprehension.

The Gentiles, according to biblical teaching, enter into the Jews' glory and inheritance only after, and on the occasion of, its rejection by the Jews. God's act of turning toward the Gentiles is also his act of turning from the Jews. The divine election of the Gentiles has as its other side the divine rejection of the Jews. If Gentile branches are grafted in, it is only after, and on the occasion of, the break-off of Jewish branches. Through Israel's fall,

31

salvation comes to the Gentiles. Gentiles are saved only after, and because, Jews are lost (Romans 11:17, 19).

Did Israel "stumble that it might fall"? Paul answers this question in vigorous language: "God forbid" (Romans 11:11). Israel's fall is not an end in itself. It did not occur for its own sake. It occurred rather for the salvation of the Gentiles (Romans 11:11).

Moreover, Paul also teaches that Gentiles have been saved not for their own sakes, but to provoke the Jews to jealousy, that they too may be saved (Romans 11:11). As the Gentiles obtained mercy through Jewish disobedience, so the Jews are to obtain mercy through the mercy shown to the Gentiles (Romans 11:31). As the Jews did not stumble for the sake of falling but rather that salvation might thereby come to the Gentiles, so Gentiles are saved not for their own sakes but for the sake of the salvation of the Jews.

Paul urges that he would not have Gentile Christians "ignorant of this mystery, lest ye be wise in your own conceits" (Roman 11:25). Unless Gentile Christians remember that they are saved through Israel's fall, and saved not for their own sakes but for the sake of the salvation of the Jews, they will fall into religious pride. "Be not high minded," Paul warns (Romans 11:20). And what is Christian anti-Semitism but pride — religious pride — the very kind of pride that kept many Jews from accepting the Christ of the gospel?

In view of this, how can the Church or the individual Gentile Christian regard the Jew with religious prejudice? Can he lay a special guilt and disobedience upon the Jew, if he and the Church have been saved through the occasion of this guilt and disobedience? And further, can he condemn those through whom and for whom he has received his redemption? Can a Christian be anti-

Semitic and reject the Jews without rejecting the gospel? Anti-Semitism is anti-gospel, and ultimately anti-Christ, for it is a rejection of God's method and means of saving the Gentile *and* the Jew. If the Gentile Christian truly understands the gospel of his salvation, he cannot judge the Jews as "most responsible" for the crucifixion of Christ without repudiating the gospel and the Lord who bought him.

Gentiles are saved, and the gospel has come to them, not apart from the Jews and their particular history, but as a part of their history. For Gentiles to reject the Jews because of their history — including their present history — is to reject Jesus Christ himself, because Christ, as does their own salvation, exists not apart from, but only in that history. Apart from that history, Christ and the salvation of the Gentiles is unintelligible. To the extent that the Church ignores the current history of the Jews, it is in danger of misunderstanding its gospel.

Instead of measuring Jewish guilt for the crucifixion, the Gentile who knows the time of his salvation will break into doxology to God. Paul saw God's historical-revelational dealings with both Jew and Greek as his method of having "mercy upon all" (Romans 11:32). Seeing this, he condemned neither Jew nor Gentile but raised the doxology: "O the depth of the riches both of the wisdom and knowledge of God!" (Romans 11:33a).

The basis of this doxology is the final, positive answer to all anti-Semitism. When the Gentile Church recognizes this and lives accordingly, she will be close to that moment in her history that will be as a resurrection from the dead: the reunion of Jew and Gentile in the oneness of the Church. For anti-Semitism hinders the Gentile's calling to provoke the Jews to jealousy.

The ecumenical movement is rightly concerned about

33

the disunity existing among the various segments of the Church. But this disunity will be overcome, as Barth reminded Evanston, only when the Church understands the gospel of Jesus Christ in a way that excludes all anti-Semitism. If the Church does not renounce anti-Semitism, it will lack that quality of spirit necessary for the achievement of the unity of all Christians.

The response that this essay elicited when first published in *Christianity Today,* and especially after it was reported in the *New York Times,* revealed that the elimination of anti-Semitism cannot be wholly successful. Even if Christians desisted from all anti-Semitism, many Jewish people would still insist that the Christian Church is anti-Semitic. It would take nothing less than the denial of the Christian faith to remove everything that some Jewish people regard as anti-Semitic.

Many Jews reject much of the New Testament record of the trial and death of Jesus Christ as unhistorical. They insist that the gospel records are a fabric of prejudice, written to put the Jews in a bad light by blaming them for what the Gentiles, specifically the Romans, are responsible. Thus when they, as does Jules Isaac, quote Christian teaching about the crucifixion, they insist on the repudiation by Christians of such views as Christians ought to reject, but they also insist on the rejection of such views and teachings as the Christian Church, true to the New Testament records, may not reject. Moreover, they often argue, as Jules Isaac does, that the Jews did not crucify the Son of God, and they seek to prove their point by asserting that Jesus never claimed to be the Son of God. There is no possible resolution of anti-Semitism if the New Testament teaching that Jesus is "God with us," that "God was in Christ" is *per se* anti-Semitic.

34

Jules Isaac sees one of the three main roots of Christian anti-Semitism in the Church's contention that the spiritual life of the Jews was degenerate at the time of Christ. He insists on its virility at that time. But from the Christian point of view, it was the very virility of the Jews' religious reaction to Christ that accounts for their insistence on his crucifixion. Unlike the Romans and the Gentiles generally, the Jews experienced the offense of the Cross. Further, the degenerate character of the Jews' spirituality is revealed precisely by their rejection and crucifixion of Christ. Jews and Christians simply differ on the evaluation of Christ, and if the Jews insist that the Christian evaluation of Christ is *per se* anti-Semitic, then there can be no relief for it. It is a peculiar blindness of Jules Isaac, who is so often very perceptive, which asserts that Christians could remove all these roots of anti-Semitism and yet not "oppose a doctrine essential to the Christian faith" (*The Teaching of Contempt,* pp. 34, 118, 119). Similarly, he claims that another basic root of anti-Semitism lies in the Christian judgment that the Diaspora and destruction of Jerusalem constitute a judgment of God upon Israel. He regards this theological judgment as historical nonsense because the Diaspora had begun long before Christ was born. The Christian Church believes that Scripture affords sufficient grounds for regarding the destruction of Jerusalem as an act of divine judgment.

Yet Isaac, and many other Jews who offer the same objections, are right in so far as they contend that the state of Jewish religious life at the time of Christ and the destruction of Jerusalem in A.D. 70 give the Church no ground for despising the Jew. And the better the Church understands this, the better she will understand her own gospel.

On the matter of the Christian assessment of the person of Christ as God in the flesh, the Jew can no more expect the Christian to surrender this, than the Christian can expect the Jew to deny his deep conviction that God is one God.

Ultimately, the only resolution of the kind of anti-Semitism that the Jew presses against the Church, which the Church cannot regard as anti-Semitism at all (and literally it is not), is that the Jew find in Christ's death that unity and peace which God establishes through the breaking down of "the wall of partition." That is to say, the resolution can only occur in the Church where both Jew and Gentile find their unity in Christ. In Christ lies the clue to the meaning of history, the history of both the Jew and the Gentile. But this will become clear only to the degree that the Church, in obedience to the gospel, ceases from every kind of authentic anti-Semitism.

2

Christian, Jew, and Negro

PEOPLE ARE PROMPTED BY SOME DEEP MORAL IMPULSE
to separate the human race into two groups. Some place
the line of separation between free, democratic societies,
and totalitarian, communistic societies.* Others place the
division between the white and the colored races, usually
between the white and the Negro. Script writers for
"Westerns" divide men into the good men and the bad
men. The Christian usually locates the division between
Christians and non-Christians — a kind of baptized version of the Western TV morality skit, and a prolific
source of self-righteousness. If the Christian is of the
Reformed tradition, he is apt to divide all humanity into
the elect and the non-elect.

* That the truly radical difference does not lie between democratic and communistic societies has profound implications on
many levels of practical life. In the area of international foreign
policy, for example, it means the rejection of those simple
solutions which appeal to abstract principles of justice and righteousness. The modern descendants within the Christian community of the New Testament "sons of thunder" who, in the
name of righteousness, would blast communism from the earth
by nuclear warfare have placed the deepest division between
mankind in the wrong place.

37

TABOR COLLEGE LIBRARY
HILLSBORO. KANSAS 67063

While the principle of division greatly varies, all divisions have this in common: the divided groups are related to each other by tension and conflict. The groups are always antithetically and competitively related, each calling for the suppression and sometimes the elimination of the other. And the meaning of history is thought to lie in this conflict.

In contrast to all the above divisions, the Bible asserts that the deepest division between men in history lies between Jew and Gentile. In biblical thought, man in sin is united against God, and to overcome this sinful unity of man in history, God introduces a division between men. It is not man, but God who inserts into history its deepest cleavage. And the purpose of God's division is quite unlike that of any of the divisions and conflicts that man introduces into history. God introduces a division and a conflict in historical humanity in order to resolve every conflict and to save the world. He seeks its unification. God divides to reconcile. Unlike the "Western," which resolves the conflict between the good men and the bad men in the last act — after innumeral commercials — by killing off the bad men, God seeks to save humanity. God seeks reconciliation, not destruction. And whereas the divisions introduced by man posit an eternal conflict so that there is, at best, no resolution except by continued suppression, or, at worst, the elimination of the opposition, the biblical conflict is for the time being, for the conflict is to be overcome and unity and peace are to be restored.

It is not man, nor even his sin, that cuts the deepest gorge in the stream of human history, but God's election of the Jewish nation, which separates the Jews from all other peoples. By virtue of its divine election, the Jewish

38

people are God's peculiar people, the people of the law and the covenant. It is this people whom God selected to be the recipients and conveyors of the knowledge of God, the light of the Gentiles, the hope of the world, the nation from whose history and life Christ would come. And as God's election of the Jews constitutes them the people of God, the people from whom God takes the name by which he will forever be known, "the God of Abraham, Isaac, and Jacob," the Gentiles in biblical thought and language are "no people"; they are "without God and without hope in the world." It is God's election of the Jews that erects between the Jews and Gentiles "a middle wall of partition," and posits between them, according to St. Paul's teaching in the New Testament, "enmity."

UNLESS THIS DIVISION IS RECOGNIZED, WE FAIL TO UNderstand the meaning and accomplishment of the Cross of Christ. For it is the Cross, according to the New Testament, that breaks down this wall of partition, resolves the enmity between Jew and Gentile, and of the two makes "one new man, so making peace." Through the Cross the two groups are reconciled and find their unity, and thereby their peace. This unity *is* the Church, the Body of Christ. For this reason the Church cannot be saved apart from the salvation of the Jewish people. Thus the Church becomes the symbol and the guarantee, both to the world and to "the principalities and the powers in the heavenly places" (Ephesians 3:10), of God's supreme purpose in history, the reconciliation and unification of all things in Christ, things visible and things invisible, things in heaven and things on earth, of this world and the next. Through the resolution of the conflict between Jew and Gentile, achieved through the Cross of Christ, the eternal purpose and design of God's will is disclosed. Every discussion of God's eternal purpose, every view of what God wants with history and will obtain through history that ignores this election of the Jewish people is simply wide of the Cross.

There is a significant passage in chapter 12 of John's Gospel that bears on this matter. After Jesus' own people had largely forsaken him just before his death, two of his disciples informed him that some Greeks desired an audience with him. The response of Jesus is striking: "Verily, verily, I say unto you, except a grain of wheat fall into the earth and die, it abideth by itself alone; but if it die, it beareth much fruit." Jesus here asserts that the separation and election of the Jewish people narrows down until he alone is on one side of the line, and all the rest of humanity, both Jews and Gentiles, are on the other side. And at the Cross Jesus is alone. No man, neither Jew nor Greek, identifies himself with Jesus. None pleads his case; no man stands with him. Here the election of the Jewish people and their separation from others is concentrated in Jesus. And men, both Jew and Roman Gentile, in their separation from him stand around the Cross and argue against his election. Nowhere are they, both Jew and Gentile, more separated from him than when they reject the election of him who alone is the ground of their election. And here, at the deepest point of separation between men, the Seed falls into the ground and, dying, is no longer alone. For as Jesus says in his discourse recorded in the same chapter, "And I, if I be lifted up from the earth, will draw all men unto myself." The basic separation between men is posited by God's elective action and falls between Gentiles and Jews, and specifically on this Jew, God's Elect. But by the death of God's *Elect,* the two are made one in

40

Christ, the enmity is resolved by the reconciling power of his Cross, and thus peace is made.

HISTORY, THEREFORE, ACCORDING TO THE BIBLICAL teaching, must be theologically interpreted: it is Christ who is the center and the meaning of history. All things in history derive their meaning and significance from the crucified Christ. But history concerns people more than things. It is especially humanity, therefore, that must be theologically interpreted; and where it is, there will be the recognition that the deepest division embedded in humanity is not between Communist and non-Communist, between good men and bad men, between white and colored, nor even between saints and sinners, nor the Church and the world. Biblical theology is not based on color, but on God's election, and the object of his election is not the white man rather than the Negro, but the Jew rather than the Gentile.

If God, as St. Paul says, is "no respecter of persons," God is even less a respecter of color. But if election has nothing to do with color, it is equally true that the biblical idea of election can never lose its Jewish character. As was said, the God of the Bible is the God of Abraham, Isaac, and Jacob and this, says God, "is my name forever." The Jews are and remain God's chosen people, "for the gifts and the calling of God are not repented of" (Romans 11:29). Jesus, as the Christ and the Elect of God, will always be the "seed of Abraham" and the "son of David."

Here lies the biblical perspective on the question of both race and election. At the Cross is disclosed the truth about race and election. Here it is revealed that the non-elect is not the Negro but the Gentile, whatever his race or color. Yet how often Christian people have

41

gone to the Old Testament to find biblical support for the specious argument that the Negro is a lesser people by virtue of a divine curse. How often the proponents of this specious argument have been Gentile Christians, members of the Christian Church. And how painfully often it has been the conservative, rather than the more liberal Christian, who has looked for such biblical support! Had he gone to the Cross for his answer, the Gentile Christian would have discovered that it is not the Negro who is the "lesser breed" but the Gentile, white or Negro, yellow or red.

In contrast to the Jew, it is the Gentile who knows not the law and is without God and without hope in the world. At the Cross the Gentile Christian can learn that there is no theological justification for anti-Jewish or Negro prejudice. On the contrary, he can learn there that in the eyes of God white and Negro are on the same side of the line, and that if either is to enter into the truth of Christianity it is by participating and sharing in the election, the glory, and the inheritance of the Jews. For without this participation, the Gentile, whatever his color, is, in biblical language, "no people."

The Cross is the center of history; only there can one gain the Christian perspective on history. There it is disclosed that the dynamics of history flow not between races or color of skin, but between Jew and Gentile. All the extant divisions between men based on race and color must be viewed in the light of this deeper division disclosed and resolved at the Cross of Calvary. When the problems of race, nationality, and color are resolved elsewhere, both the election of God and the Cross of Christ have been ignored.

This is only a thumbnail sketch of the biblical understanding of history and race, yet it would be well if we kept even this little in view lest we become so fixed on the lesser divisions that subdivide mankind that we lose the Christian perspective.

Caught in the profound and convulsive movements of change and revolution that mark our time, we are apt to forget that the secret of history is still a theological one. If we have forgotten, we may indeed be surprised in the future to discover that the religious tensions in America are fraught with even greater powers of disruption and bitterness than is the racial issue that has captured public attention. And the future may disclose that the stirrings in the Israeli-Arab world are far more decisive for the future history of the world than the movements of World Communism.

It is the Cross, not the Kremlin, Peking, or the Ku Klux Klan, that holds the secret of history. The Church cannot afford to forget that her gospel is by biblical definition in its very nature "for the Jew first," and then, and only then, for the Gentile. Nor can the Church afford to forget that she *is* that unity which Christ has achieved in history, and that her very existence and function are to be a witness of that ultimate unity of all peoples and all things which it is God's eternal purpose to realize in Christ.

The Church is the product of the reconciling work of the Cross. There, at the Cross, she must live, and there gauge every wind of change that blows, for only there can she gain the biblical perspective on every revolution of history.

WE ARE LIVING IN A TIME OF SOCIAL REVOLUTION UN-equaled in the history of the world. The race issue in the United States, and the world across, is only one aspect of this revolution. Yet in so far as people, rather than

43

science or any such thing, make history, the racial revolution is of tremendous significance. Progress has indeed been made, and we in the United States may be thankful for the passage of the 1964 Civil Rights Bill. Yet this forward move may prove to be the easiest part of the long road to be traveled. Christians who advise that we must not move too fast in giving the Negro his civil rights ought to consider rather with what speed a Christian should return to the Cross. Moreover, the Negro, like the white man, lives only once; once the Negro is over the Jordan, he will not need the benefits of civil rights. Nor will his child be able to do anything with an equal opportunity for education after he is past school age.

Are we moving too fast? In the eleven deep-South states, and the bordering states, the average increase in school integration during the ten years since the Supreme Court's decision of 1954 is *one* percent. We can hardly expect the Negro to accept a pace that will take one hundred years, not to achieve integration, but to undo an illegal segregation.

A word should also be said about those, both Christian and non-Christian, who seek to impede the enactment of civil rights legislation on federal and state levels by urging that "morals cannot be legislated." This argument has no visible means of support and is only the more transparently specious when urged in the name of morality and piety. Christians who support the claim that morals cannot be legislated, by appealing to the fact that man's greatest need is faith in Christ and regeneration by his Spirit, are uttering a very dangerous half-truth. They are surely right about the individual man's greatest need, but they are as surely wrong when they contend that men's moral and social behavior cannot be

44

improved by legislation. For what other reason does society have laws against theft, murder, rape, and other kinds of criminal behavior? Does anyone advocate the elimination of such laws? The truth that legislation furthers morality is so clear that only eyes blinded by prejudice can fail to see it.

Furthermore, while man's ultimate good demands faith and becoming a new creature in Christ, it is manifest untruth that the spiritual regeneration of men is the condition on which prejudice will automatically vanish. Some of the strongholds of racial prejudice are found within the Christian Church itself and in those parts of the United States where the Church is most conservative.

Christians who urge that morals cannot be legislated and press the specious argument that racial prejudice simply melts when men become new creatures in Christ ignore not only the facts of life but also the plain facts of biblical teaching. To whom did the Ten Commandments come and to whom the civil legislation of the Old Testament? To the people of the Covenant who lived in the sphere of God's grace and Spirit. In biblical thought, the Law came *after* the Covenant, and only to the Covenant people. Who but the Christian can *properly* love his neighbor *as he loves himself?* The obvious answer, however, also points up the fact that the Law was given to, because needed by, the Christian.

In biblical thought, law serves the purposes of grace and for that very reason morality *can be legislated.* And it does not take the eyes of faith to see this. A century ago slavery was accepted by many people in both the South and the North, both in and outside the Christian Church. Slavery in the United States was then *outlawed,* and today not even the most rabid racist is expressing a desire for the return of slavery. Morals can be

45

legislated. One can only hope and pray that the children of light will see what some of the children of darkness have long seen.

IN AUGUST OF 1963, TWO HUNDRED THOUSAND NEGROES marched not *on* but *in* Washington. They marched not with guns but in protest. They walked the short distance from the Washington Monument to the Lincoln Memorial. The route was appropriate. The street down which they marched bears the name Constitution Avenue. On stones that almost cried out, they sang and waved banners, and under the brooding figure of Lincoln, America's most visited historic site until John F. Kennedy was laid to rest, they made speeches to man and prayed to God.

The District of Columbia was afraid — as were the area residents of Maryland and Virginia. People stayed home. Instead of the usual snarled traffic in the District, the streets were quiet — as on an early Sunday morning. Business was off eighty to ninety percent. The day before the historic Washington March this writer caught his usual ride from Arlington into the District. As the car in which he rode approached the District, the driver, a dignified elderly gentleman and bank manager, suddenly leaned over, opened the glove compartment, and took out a revolver. "It hasn't been fired in forty years," he said, "but I am getting bullets for it today." Fear had driven peaceful people to make preparations to pull a trigger. As the day passed and night came, fears grew. That same night this writer went to the area where the March was to begin. He soon found a microphone thrust his way and then heard himself predict that there would be "no serious trouble." As the night wore on and tension mounted, he regretted his little-shared optimism. The

46

Army had men and equipment strategically located for instant dispersal.

But the day came and went, and there was no violence. Members of George Lincoln Rockwell's Nazi Bund were there, like other creepy creatures that come crawling out from under stones, to feed on the occasion. But they were immediately surrounded by the police, their would-be speaker arrested, and the lot of them dispersed even before the March began. There was no violence. The two hundred thousand marchers were orderly and polite, apologizing for even the slightest social infraction of good manners. The owner of a bumped elbow received a gracious and sincere apology.

The moral dimensions of this historic sign of social revolution were as tall as the Washington Monument. The marchers stole the conscience of the nation. Their moral protest was a glowing tribute to their character and to their Negro leadership. It was a historic march, an event of such moral quality as one rarely sees in human history. There was something Christlike in the patient restraint of long-endured pain and injustice, and something reminiscent of "Father, forgive them" in this people who though long reviled, reviled not again. One thought of earlier Americans and their response to a tax on tea: although these marchers and their children had suffered from the law's long delay, they were not summoning men to armed revolution, nor calling down fire from heaven. They did not seek to eliminate the white man; they besought from the white man and from God only the right to join the white American and his way of life. There were no threats. But there was quiet intent, and unconcealed determination. The March was short, but no march ever gained so much. The sound of moving feet, echoing the pain and hurt of the Negro soul sobbed out in American spirituals and folksongs, will linger on in the historical memory of the American people.

If the moral dimensions of the March were as tall as the Washington Monument, the brooding over justice denied through long delay was as somber and awesome as that expressed in the face of Lincoln enshrined in his historic monument. The Negroes gave quiet notice that they wanted their legal, democratic American rights, and they wanted them now. Their patience revealed a controlled impatience. They publicly sought by non-violence and the due processes of law the rights that honest men cannot deny are theirs by every American tradition. They appealed to the consciences of their suppressors. Convinced that no man has a right to set the timetable for another man's freedom, they wanted their freedom now. All of it. They conveyed the just thought that they would not be satisfied by a slow, gradual reception of the rights that they and their fathers and grandfathers should never have been denied. They appealed peaceably to America, to its conscience, and to the traditions for which it stands: to liberty and justice for all. But like true Americans, they intimated that there were limits beyond which injustice need not be suffered. They indicated that they do not intend to wait another hundred years. And what true American, who glories in the spirit of 1776, can blame them?

What does it all mean? As the ballad of our social revolution goes, "The answer, my friend, is blowing in the wind." If the American people are unwilling to live by their own political beliefs and traditions, if they proclaim freedom abroad but refuse to implement the Civil Rights Bill of 1964, if the South and the ghetto sections of the North are unwilling to read the social signs of our times, what was peaceful, public, non-violent, may

48

well become sullen, bitter, non-public and violent. Wild revenge and frustrated acts of reprisal could easily replace the mood of a Mrs. Medgar Evers, who publicly on that memorable August day in Washington asked that there be no hatred for the shotgun destruction of her husband one hate-filled night.

THE CHURCH IN THE UNITED STATES, ALREADY SHAMED by the integrated U. S. military services and the Brooklyn, now Los Angeles, Dodgers, will regain a knowledge of its own nature only if as a predominantly Gentile Church it will recall that it, too, was once "no people" and was "once upon a time," with the Negro, outside the pale of God's election and "without God and without hope in the world"! If only she will finally recognize this, then she may be moved by those theological and religious considerations that lie far deeper than the color of skin, and she may read the signs of the time as a call to repentance and reform. The liberal American churches had their social gospel and the evangelical churches their Bible, yet both long remained insensitive to the most obvious blight and the greatest social injustice on the American social scene. Indeed, if the Church can recognize that the reduced social status of the American Negro is for the Church something far greater than a gross social injustice, namely a violation of every fundamental truth of her faith and confession, then there is hope that the Church can and will act in accordance with her nature.

There are twenty-two million Negroes in America. With them we are caught in the winds of social change that blow across our land and the world, winds that will not be stayed, because their time is come. Justice for the Negro has been long suppressed and delayed, but the day will surely come when the moral pressure of right becomes greater than the evil that suppresses it, and justice will explode like the wrath of God. It will do so because it *is* the wrath of God. Responsible Negro leaders do not say what will happen if little is done to right ancient evil. They simply continue to say, as Martin Luther King, recent winner of the Nobel Peace Prize, said in a speech that may well go down in the annals of great American oratory, "I had a dream." They may simply quote spirituals, which have a threatening dimension by their very appeal to the God of justice. When James Baldwin chose from the words "God gave Noah the rainbow sign; no more water, the fire next time" a title for one of his books, he may, to his own surprise, have been preaching his greatest sermon.

Freedom moves through the land. The God of justice moves across the earth. We Americans, and especially we who are in the Church, can ignore the answer that blows in the wind only to our hurt and shame. I say especially the Church, for if America falls under the justice of God for its failure to live by the justice of which it is the brightest example in the earth, the memory of her past will die with her. But the Church will live on — haunted by the memory of her sins and failures. The agency of God's grace, the Church surely must know that it is the nature of grace to be just *and* to move beyond justice. As God can be gracious only after he has recognized the demands of justice, the Church can speak of God's grace only after she has recognized the claims of justice.

If the Church proclaims the grace of the gospel while she rejects the very justice on which grace can alone be gracious, she is denying the very gospel she proclaims.

Both Protestants and Roman Catholics have been very

slow to respond to the cancer of racial discrimination and prejudice. In early 1963, in Chicago, both groups met for the first time with Jewish leaders for a Conference on Religion and Race. Called one hundred years to the month after President Lincoln's Declaration of Emancipation had freed the U. S. Negro slave, the Chicago meeting was the *first* such effort, on a national basis, to see what could be done to marshal the energies of the three groups against America's most glaring social injustice.

Protestants, Roman Catholics, and Jews agreed at this conference that racism is a violation of their common understanding of man's creation in the image of God. As such, it is an affront to God himself. All were embarrassed at their past failures to lift up their voice against this national disgrace. And each was embarrassed most by the continuing discrimination found within its own religious group.

Eager for publicity for their belated efforts, the Protestants, Catholics, and Jews called a meeting of the secular and religious press. But the embarrassment was poignant as the uneasy leadership of the three groups was questioned by the members of the *secular* press whether the Christian churches and the Jewish synagogues did not exercise discipline upon members guilty of the balder forms of racial discrimination. The religious press knew better than to ask such questions, but the secular press in its naive integrity assumed that the churches and synagogues were disciplined communities.

Pressed by the secular press men, the religious leadership of the various groups had to admit that racial discrimination existed not only among their respective memberships, but also within the *very structures* of the ecclesiastical establishments. These confessions conceded

51

that racial discrimination was not only officially practiced but was also officially condoned. The secular press was gracious, for none of the reporters carried the confessions in the stories they wrote for their papers.

Here is a profound weakness in many of America's churches: many of them exercise no formal discipline upon their members. Membership usually comes easy, and one would have to work hard at unbelief to lose it. In the more liberal churches a member can deny the deity of Christ, his virgin birth, his bodily resurrection, the reality of hell, the doctrine of the trinity, and the finality of the Christian religion without jeopardizing his membership. Nor is his behavior, or misbehavior, likely to threaten his membership status. Except for the act of suicide, it is almost impossible to sin one's way out of membership in many churches.

But let a member of such a church, or of a conservative church for that matter, do something that threatens the ecclesiastical establishment, or its leadership, and disciplinary action will come sure and swift. Sins of unbelief or conduct that threaten the truth of Christ and the Christian religion will be shown great tolerance, but anything that threatens the religious establishment, or its leadership, will touch a sensitivity that protects its honor with a speed akin to lightning and with a heaviness akin to the wrath of God.

With rare exceptions, usually found in the smaller denominations, the churches of America are undisciplined. A recent poll conducted by the Research Center of the University of California at Berkeley, California, revealed that there are thousands of atheists and thousands who do not believe in a life after death among the membership of some of the larger American denominations. If atheists cannot last in foxholes, they can ap-

52

parently abide in church pews. Although Jesus said, "Fear him that is able to cast both body and soul into hell," bullets seem to teach more to the atheists in foxholes than do sermons to atheist church members in the pew.

Whenever the churches move to protect their established and institutionalized interest, they show that they do possess a regulatory power over their memberships. They have, however, been singularly negligent about exercising it in the areas of Christian belief and practice.

If any church has disciplined a member to the point of exclusion from membership for even the grossest forms of racial prejudice, it is not generally known to the public. Yet many churches have engaged in racial demonstrations and called loudly for a federal civil rights bill. Such actions would seem far more natural and commendable if these same churches had applied the moral force of Christian discipline to their own membership guilty of un-Christian racial prejudice and behavior. But failing this, when these same churches engage in civil rights demonstrations, make noble high-level ecclesiastical pronouncements, call for quick implementation of the federal civil rights bill, they create for themselves an ambiguous public image. Moreover, when the churches appeal to the Federal Government to achieve that simple justice for the Negro which they have as yet not achieved among their own membership by that divine grace of which they as churches claim to be agents, they create the public impression that law can achieve what grace cannot. Law is made to appear stronger than grace, and the secular state able to do for all Americans what the American churches cannot achieve even within their own membership.

Thus the actions of the churches calling for political and social justice in this situation are in fact a denial of the gospel and of what the churches claim to be. Whenever the Church must appeal to the State to accomplish among all kinds of men what it has not accomplished among its own membership, it has weakened its claim to be the Church and has rendered unto Caesar the things that belong to God.

3

At the Cross

IN ITS TEACHING AND PREACHING THE CHRISTIAN CHURCH has made much of the mockery that Jesus suffered on the Cross. And rightly so. The Cross was a place of derision, a scene of mockery. According to the New Testament records, "The rulers scoffed at him." "They that passed by railed on him." "The soldiers also mocked him." The malefactor "railed on him." And "in like manner also the chief priests mocked, with the scribes and elders."

But why did even those who merely "passed by" rail on him? Why was the scorn so withering? Why was the derision so biting, the railing so bitter? What accounts for this cruelty of spirit, these heartless, merciless words to one in the anguish of dying? What hidden truth gives scorn so cruel an edge, contempt so sharp a tongue?

A cross, some nails: men had died this way before. Yet the mockery, if any, had then been less eloquent, and the derision without this dimension of depth. At these others times some sympathy had often mingled with hard duty. Why at the Cross of Christ is the scorn and disdain so wide and deep, so unrelieved? Who is this Jesus, the object of this mockery?

The answer, according to the New Testament, is clear enough. Jesus had claimed to be the Christ, God's Elect, the one chosen of God. It was this claim of being God's Elect that elicited the unequaled depths of scorn and ridicule, even from a people that itself claimed to be God's elect people, his chosen nation.

This mockery of Jesus' election was as essential a part of the crucifixion as were the nails and the noon-day darkness. The mockery of Jesus was mankind's reaction to God's election. Mankind nailed Jesus to the Cross because he claimed to be God's Elect, and thereby mankind revealed what it thought of God's election. The Cross was mankind's rejection of God's election.

IT HAS OFTEN ESCAPED NOTICE THAT THE MEN AT THE foot of the Cross talked theology. They discussed one thing only: the theology of election. It was the sole topic of their conversation, and in terms of Jesus' claim to be God's Elect they appraised his crucifixion. In their mockery and scoffing, the chief priests, the scribes and the elders, and the malefactor are giving their answer to Jesus' claim that though forsaken of God and rejected, he is nonetheless God's Elect. They cry in derision: "He trusted in God; let him deliver him now, if he desireth him." If Jesus, they say, is the one whom God desires above all others, let it be demonstrated by an act of divine deliverance. If this is the one whom God wishes to have for himself, the one in whom he delights and is well pleased, if this one is the good pleasure of God, then let God indicate his choice and preference by rescuing him from the jaws of death. If he is truly God's Elect, God will save him — or Elijah will come down to aid him — and then, say they, we will believe that he is what he claims to be.

With an irony born from a ridicule of his claim to be God's chosen, they cry in derision: "He saved others; let him save himself, if this is the Christ of God, his chosen!" "And the soldiers also mocked him, coming to him, offering him vinegar, and saying, If thou art the King of the Jews, save thyself." "And one of the malefactors that were hanged railed on him, saying, Art not thou the Christ? save thyself and us." "In like manner also the chief priests, mocking, with the scribes and elders said, . . . Let him now come down from the cross, and we will believe on him."

If God, or Elijah, intervenes to save him, or if he is able to save himself from the Cross, they will believe that he is God's Elect. But if nothing happens and he dies, then God has rejected him and his claim, for according to the Jewish Scriptures, "Cursed is every one that hangeth on a tree." When God in his providence allows Jesus to die on the Cross, they know he is cursed and rejected by God. They recognized his rejection, but not his election.

THUS THE JEWS AT THE CROSS MISUNDERSTOOD THE RE-jection of Jesus. They misunderstood it because they did not acknowledge his election. Only in the light of Jesus' election can his rejection be understood. He was elected to be rejected. And this is only to say that the Cross can be understood only in terms of Christ's election. On their view of election, and of their own election, which they countered against Jesus' claim, Jesus was not the Christ, the chosen one of God, for the Elect should prosper; he should live, not die. Yet mistaken though they were, they rightly perceived that the meaning of the Cross turned on the question of the election and rejection of

Jesus — and they spoke, in mockery, of nothing else. Though they misconstrued the issue, they knew what the issue was.

How profoundly those who mocked misunderstood the election of Jesus — and their own! Precisely because he was God's Elect, he could not come down from the Cross; he could not save himself, could not preserve his life, could not live by the principles of "safety first," of "self-preservation," and "self-interest." Because he was God's Elect, he must die as the one rejected by God. Any word, any movement to save himself, would have announced that he was not the Christ, the one above all others chosen of God.

As God's Elect, Jesus is God's Servant. "Behold my servant whom I have chosen, my elect in whom my soul delighteth." As the one, he is the other. If he were not the Servant, he would not be God's Elect. As God's elected Servant he must die on the Cross for others. As the one chosen by God to be rejected by God, he is God's Servant; he must not save but lose his life for others. This is the disclosure that he is God's Servant, the Elect of God, the Christ.

IT IS HERE THAT THE JEWS MUST UNDERSTAND THE nature and meaning of their own election. For Israel herself, according to her ancient Scriptures, is God's Servant, the nation in whom God delighted (and still delights), God's chosen people. And it is only when the Jewish people understand their election at the Cross that they will understand their election aright. Then they will also understand the Pauline teaching that they are now partially, and for the time being, rejected by God for the salvation of the Gentiles. When this disclosure of the meaning of the election and rejection of

Jesus falls as a light upon their mind, their mockery will turn into praise, and their ridicule into the Pauline doxology: O the height and depth both of the wisdom and the knowledge of God!

When this occurs, the Jewish people will understand that the meaning of their entire history is grounded in Jesus Christ, which is to say, the meaning of their election (and temporary rejection) is grounded in and derived from the election and rejection of Jesus Christ. For apart from the Christ of the Cross, the entire history of this nation, and the individual experiences of the individual Jew, including election and rejection, are meaningless.

In a quite similar way this is also true about the Christian Church. She, too, will never understand her election except in terms of the election of Christ, nor her need to bear the Cross and live for others except in terms of his rejection and crucifixion. For the nature and meaning of the Church's election — including that of the individual Christian — are grounded in the election of Christ as he appears in his crucifixion. From God's Chosen One on the Cross, the Church's election derives her meaning and her calling and service to the world. For the election of the Church, her calling and service, indeed her entire history — as also that of the individual Christian — has no meaning except as it is grounded in and derives its purpose and significance from the crucifixion of God's Elect.

HOW CONTRARY TO SCRIPTURE, YET HOW COMMON, IS the misunderstanding of election displayed by those who were at the Cross but not on it. How prevalent the notion that to be God's elect is to be established in life, to prosper, to be protected and rendered safe. Election is often regarded as a kind of insurance policy that insures success and well-being. How little it is understood that to be God's elect is to be called not "to be ministered unto" but "to minister," not to save one's life but to lose it. How little we accept the fact that to be God's elect does not mean in the first instance to be saved, but the opposite — to go to the Cross, to be crucified with Christ, to lose one's life for the sake of the gospel in the service of others.

Election is a call to service, though not necessarily a prolonged service: it may be a call to one final act of service. Election is a call to the service of the Cross, to self-denial and self-sacrifice; a summons to take up one's cross, to participate in the sufferings and the duties of the drama of redemption, to fulfill, as Paul says, the sufferings of Christ. It is a call to take no thought for one's life what one shall eat or what one shall drink in order to sustain one's life and guarantee a future. It is a call to spend one's life for others, to be "for the world," even when one is rejected by the world.

Election is a call to live and die, "to be set at nought" for others in claims of the gospel of the Cross, to lose all, and after all is lost, then to be saved by receiving one's life back again as a gift of grace in a better resurrection. The elect must always refuse to save themselves — not only in the ultimate sense but also in that ordinary sense in which one can lose his life every day. Not to be willing fully to do so is to sin against one's election.

The critical question is not to ask in the abstract, apart from the Cross, whether I *am* one of God's elect, but whether in terms of the Cross I am *willing* to be one of his elect. When election is understood at the Cross of Christ, the critical question is whether the individual and the Church are willing to take their everyday hopes and dreams, their ordinary religious ideas and ideals, their own guarantees for the future, and nail them to the Cross. For there is no knowledge, no under-standing, and no assurance of election except at the foot of the Cross, where the Elect of God shows what election is.

4

The Glory of God

EVERYMAN TOILS TO AMOUNT TO SOMETHING, AND THEN
adds toil to add something to the amount. In the interest of increase, Everyman strains his body and stretches
his mind, and even bends his ethics and compromises
his convictions.

Everyman has a reputation to build. And the build-
ing must be constantly enlarged as a protection against
the competitive successes of his like-minded fellows.
The pursuit of success is an ever-accelerating treadmill.
At birth he was given a name, but he turns the gift
into a task; his name must be carved large in the reluctant respect of his friends, and especially of his
enemies.

To become Somebody, Everyman must strive relent-
lessly. For each little victory and each achievement adds
something to the total, to the final sum, and the sum
must be large. For Everyman must construct an equation, an equation in which Everyman equals greatness.

And it is in this manner that Everyman becomes a
Nobody with a success that does not distinguish and a
name that does not long identify. For in the divine

economy self-seeking and work-righteousness do not long endure nor much avail. It is the meaning of grace that the works and the worker of the law must be set at nought. If Everyman is to glory, he will have to glory in the Lord; if he is to have a name that identifies and endures, he must receive it as a gift of grace. For names, like places in history and in the memory of God, are given, not taken.

THE SON OF MAN, TOO, MUST BE SET AT NOUGHT, IF HE is to receive a name that is to be remembered. He, too, must construct an equation. He must suffer, empty himself, and so serve others that they regard him as a servant. He must forget his own name, forsake his own glory. For him the ladder of success leads downward. One rung lower, and still another. The Lord of all must come in servant-form. He must command no respect, and lose such respect as he has. He must toil to become nameless. He must go to that place where a man's name and his place, as the Psalmist said, are remembered no more. He must die that God may give him a name, a name higher than that of his fellows. He must not prize highly his crown with its halo of glory. He must climb downward to the thorns and the darkness. By his own efforts he must construct an equation. He must make himself into an equation with zero; he must make himself equal to nothing. "And how is it written of the Son of Man, that he should suffer many things and be set at nought?" (Mark 9:12). For God calls to himself and God gives a name only to the things that are not. Only they who die know the resurrection.

And all this must not just happen to him. He himself must cause it to happen. He may not be a victim; even in reducing himself to zero, he must be the Lord. For

63

it is the Lord who must be equated with nothing. And if he is indeed the Lord, then only he can do it. His task is to make himself a servant. He must not be ministered unto. He must minister to others by first ministering to himself. The Lord must be his own servant, for it is the Lord of glory that must be crucified. He must empty himself, must get himself down; he must alienate his friends, his Church, and offend his disciples so that all keep their distance. He must disown his own mother. He himself must choose his Cross, determine the fact and set the time of his own death. His death is his own act. He must cause himself to be disrobed and thus be both the fulfiller and fulfillment of prophecy. He must pour out his own life in death. None can take it from him; none can render him even this service. He himself must fulfill God's word that he, the Christ, be set at nought, for only thus is he God's Word. He must build his own equation, set himself at nought, himself make himself equal to nothing.

And in it all, he must know that this is God's will for him, God's word upon him. It is God who condemns him through Pilate. The game of prophecy played upon his back is scheduled by God. The nails, the thorns, the game of dice, the disrobing are the fulfillment of God's word and will. And in it all he must thank and praise his God, and love his Father, the Father who forsakes his only Son. For while he is set at nought and reduced to nothing, he must praise the greatness of God and declare that God alone is great, the God whose will sets him at nought. Reduced to nothing, he must love God above all. When the Father curses the Son, the Son must bless the name of the Father. At the depth of suffering and agony, at the bottom of hell, he must build an altar and render worship, loving God with all his heart and mind and strength, and his neighbor as himself. At the moment when God reduces him to nothing, he must declare and confess that God is all — and in all. He must bless the heart and hand that wills this awful equation for him, and cry: Amen, so let it be, for so, Father, it is good in thy sight.

It is thus the Servant becomes the Son of Man, the Man of eschatological kingdom, power, and glory. By emptying himself, he becomes the one in whom God will sum up all things, whether in heaven or earth. By becoming nameless, so that God can give him a name, he obtains a name which is above every name, that at the name of Jesus, Everyman should bow and Everyman confess that he is Lord of lords, and King of kings. By becoming less than the birds which have nests and less than the foxes which have holes and by not having a place to lay his head, he receives a place of honor and power at God's right hand.

HOW COMFORTING TO REMEMBER THAT CHRIST WHO was rich for our sakes became poor, that he did for us what we could not do for ourselves, since we in our sin want to be as God — or, rather, as we think God is. And how comforting to learn at Calvary that God is like Christ, who was willing to become nothing and to be set at nought for our sakes.

But how comfortable to forget that the pattern of Christ's life and death is the pattern God has set for our lives. How convenient to ignore that what we could not do for ourselves is now the pattern of what we must do for him!

Being now justified by his blood, how easy to continue to build up our own image that others may confess our names; how easy to enlarge the blueprints of our prestige for the greater enhancement of our own reputations. How painless it is for the Christian to repudiate Darwinianism and the while to live by the principle of self-preservation. How tempting for the Body to become an institution of power and glory, forgetting that its Head is Lord only because he is a Servant. How easy for ecclesiastics to use the Church as a private instrument of personal power, forgetting that the Church is by definition that for which Christ was set at nought. How bloodless the effort of forgetting that Everyman who would save his life must lose it, and that only he who would lose his life for Christ's sake and the gospel shall find it.

It requires no effort to admit and even to proclaim that the Christ who was set at nought is God's infallible Word and forthwith in a lovelessness that knows no mercy to dispose of the life or reputation of others, if by so doing we may attain unto the equation of greatness. How painless to give consent to the proposition that we must be set at nought, all the while seeking to prevent the word of the Lord from coming to pass. How easy to agree that Christ is the pattern and that the call is to take up our cross and follow him, all the while reaching for the crown instead of the cross and following hard after every fragment of honor and recognition that society or some person or institution may proffer. How self-satisfying to approve civil rights for the Negro, and for every minority group in America, and yet to deny them common civility in life's common ways. For what is white racism but regarding non-whites as a lesser breed, denying in practice that they, too, are those for whom Christ was set at nought.

To be set at nought, to set oneself at nought — how exceedingly difficult! How hard to sell all that one has and to follow Jesus, to tread the road that he trod, to show a Christlike unconcern for one's own name. How much easier to follow the policy of practical prudence and careful calculation so that all men will speak well of us, while we ignore the word of the Lord that we must become as nothing before God and man. How safe to follow the instinct of self-preservation — to cry against the evil that the masses hate, but to remain silent about that which our hearts condemn, because the masses are silent.

YET GOD WILL SET EVERYMAN AT NOUGHT, FOR HE IS determined that no flesh shall glory in his sight. Everyman is obliged to believe in election, in salvation by grace alone. He is summoned to become as nothing — without falling into the pride that this will save him and make him great. Everyman must believe that not all his tears and sighs and prayers will grant him acceptance and peace with God. For only in the way of being as nothing before God will God raise him into the heavenly glory and give him a new name. If we are not merely willing to, but actually do lose our lives, we will find them again in a better resurrection. For the resurrection follows not the willingness to die, but the act of death.

And what of those races, persons, institutions, nations, and cultures that proudly refuse to become as nothing before God? They shall nonetheless be reduced to nothing. God will not punish their sin less severely than he punished it in his own Son. All worldly wisdom and power within Christendom and outside of it, in the Church, and especially within the Church, God will bring to nought. In the battle between human pride and God's glory, the outcome is not uncertain. God is determined that no flesh shall glory in his sight.

If any will glory, he will have to glory in the Lord, for when history ends and life is done, there will be nothing else in which to glory!

Jesus Christ crucified discloses the glory of God. Not in spite of, but precisely in, being set at nought Christ reveals God's glory. For the glory of God is the glory of his grace and love. God's glory is his being for others; he will therefore set at nought the self-seeking glory of Everyman.

5

The New Morality

THE GARMENT OF U.S. MORALS IS NOT SAGGING AT THE
hemline; it is coming apart at the seams. What shows
beneath is not stuff for ethical debate, but a raw violence
and unbanked disrespect that drives decent men to a
fearful concern for the very existence of men and things.
And so various national magazines have drawn the ugly
picture of wanton U.S. moral behavior and looked to
the causes that make it so. One of them, *Look* magazine,
has asked whether the Church has failed, and whether
we perhaps need a new moral code.

The first question cannot be answered simply. The
Church can hardly assert that she has not failed. Yet
she has a right to have the shape of her failure understood. She does not admit to the kind of failure *Look*
has in mind, for she disowns *Look's* understanding of
her task. She has neither the task nor the power to
insure a high moral national behavior apart from an
acceptance of her gospel which, she contends, is the
sole basis on which morality can flourish and be sus-
tained. Indeed, the Church has a right to disown a
general responsibility for current moral behavior in the

U.S. On the contrary, the Church has the duty to point out that God in our time is demonstrating that where Christian truth is widely rejected, Christian standards of morality cannot long endure. If the Church is failing, it is failing to make clear what *Look* and other national magazines turned moral analysts do not understand: that Christian morality is grounded in Christian truth about God and man, and empowered by the Spirit of Christ who is that truth.

Do we need a new moral code? This second question is only an extension of the initial misunderstanding, for morality is not fired by the demands of law but by the power of grace. Moral codes do not produce inner moral compliance. If the Church has failed here, her failure is that she has not made plain that true morality is founded on true religion, and that her message is not a moralistic but a redemptive-religious one.

The question, moreover, reveals the internal confusion within *Look's* moral stance. Is the plea actually a plea for a new moral code? If so, does not the old moral code of the Western world, the Ten Commandments, cover the issues involved? Of all the forms of immorality that concern *Look*, is any one of them outside the moral coverage of the Ten Commandments? It may be said without hesitation that none is.

Or are *Look* and other national magazines that have exposed U.S. morals looking for another, new moral code that would condone current U.S. moral behavior? Apparently not, for concern is expressed over our moral breakdown. What our national magazines seemingly want is a new moral code that will save us from our sagging morals and empower the American people to such moral decency and respect as will not menace the welfare of men and things. But then these concerned analysts of the American moral scene are not really asking for a new moral code but for such moral power as will enable people to live morally. What they want is not a code but grace, not a new morality but a return to the Christian religion.

Amid such confusion about morality and religion the task of the Church is clear; she must proclaim that the desired power does not reside in an ethical or moral code but in that spiritual power of renewal that comes through true religion. What is desired for moral amendment is the power that resides only in the divine grace conveyed through the gospel. The Church must show that as grace precedes law, so religion has precedence over morality. The wide-scale breakdown of morality in our time is a demonstration in our national life that a moral code cannot be kept apart from the grace of the gospel.

Ministers of the American churches may understandably be discouraged that even the most intelligent sector of the American people still does not understand these elementary truths about the Church's gospel, about morality and religion. But the situation should challenge and move them to make the relationship between morality and religion clear.

ONE MIGHT WITH SOME POINT ASK WHETHER THE breakdown of conventional moral standards in American life does not stem in part from the fact that many Americans have already adopted a new moral code. There is at least one class of Americans who no longer accept the moral dictates that come from Sinai and the New Testament. Rather, they accept those that come from the front office of the large corporations for which they work. Much has been written about the organizational man who in the working portion of his life allows

71

the organization in which he works to be his conscience and moral guide.

Adolf Eichmann was not an American, yet he was a frightening but apt example of the organizational man who hands over his conscience to an organization and then with a loyalty devoid of moral feeling does whatever the organization tells him to do. The transference of one's conscience to another is moral suicide. Having committed moral suicide by handing over his conscience to the Nazi political organization, Eichmann could obediently and without moral pain accept the party's directive to destroy millions of Jewish men, women, and children. Consistent with this moral abdication, on being brought to trial he felt no personal guilt or moral responsibility for attempting to exterminate the Jewish people in gas chambers.

The world stood aghast at Eichmann's moral insensitivity. Among the shocked were many organizational men who in the world of business success had allowed corporations to be their conscience, men who regarded their unqualified loyalty to such institutions as prudence, if not virtue. The recent moral abdication of some executives of large American corporations who controlled prices, eliminated competition, and rigged bids because of the demands of corporation interests, differs from Eichmann's only in that the consequences were less frightening. The initial act of allowing an organization to be one's conscience was in each case the same. The greatest culpability of these executives was not the actions for which they were brought to trial, but the initial willingness to permit an organization to decide for them what is morally right and what is morally wrong.

Nothing is more immoral, not even dishonesty or murder, than the act that seeks to escape the demands of morality by allowing something else, a political, business, ecclesiastical, or any other kind of organization to be one's conscience. Billy Graham revealed a perceptive sensitivity to the demands of Christian ethics when he asserted that the greatest thing that could happen to the cause of Christianity was not the conversion of Khrushchev but a return to integrity. Socrates was willing to follow his conscience even if it meant death for himself. Eichmann was willing to surrender his conscience to a political organization even if it meant the death of millions of Jewish men, women, and children.

Neither Eichmann nor the American business executives are thieves or murderers in the ordinary sense of the terms. It is doubtful that Eichmann ever killed anyone either before or after his Jewish assignment. Nor would the American executives referred to above steal your wallet had they the opportunity. Yet each could fall into these evils because they had first committed the graver evil of personal moral abdication and the transference of their conscience to an organization. Once this had happened, almost anything could happen in the name of loyalty to the party or institution — unless arrested by a higher moral code.

Although the world stood aghast at Eichmann and Christendom still pays its respect to the moral integrity of that "glorious pagan" Socrates, the most regrettable forms of moral surrender occur within the Church. The Old Testament prophets stood outside the organized religion of their time, but the minister of the gospel is part and parcel of the organized Church. How often he becomes an "ecclesiastic," bearing little resemblance to an Old Testament Amos or Jeremiah! Either frightened or seduced by such considerations as his next call, his salary or tenure, his promotion within the denominational hierarchy, his own morality becomes a mere echo of his denomination. Whatever the demands of status and promotion in his particular denominational organization, these become the moral imperatives of his ministry. If greater future successes call for conformity, he will conform with his church, right or wrong. All too often it is not God who is the Lord of the churchman's conscience but those standards of conformity which seem to promise advancement.

What the situation of the various types of organization men demands is not a new moral code, but an acceptance and compliance with the moral code that has long been acknowledged as adequate in the Christian West.

Had Eichmann governed his conduct by the conventional Christian code, he would rather have died than do what he did. But if an organization may function as a conscience for an individual, then neither the Western world nor the Jews themselves have a case against Eichmann or against any man who accepts the governance of the organizational conscience.

CHRISTIAN MORALITY IS BASED ON THE PROPOSITION THAT some things must be accepted as morally right and some as morally wrong because God has revealed them to be right or wrong. At Buchenwald, where thousands of Jews met death in gas chambers, there was a sign: *Hier gibt es kein Gott*: Here there is no God. This sign was not incidental to the moral standards of Buchenwald. Whenever moral standards are arrived at by rationalizations and human calculations, we have a morality without God.

This is not to suggest that biblically given moral standards are irrational or unrelated to man's best welfare. But it is to affirm that man without revelation of the good is not capable of determining what is morally good and in his own best interests. The Christian claim is that God meets this need of man by revealing basic moral principles of right and wrong, principles that man is not capable of discovering for himself. Here lies the need and the function of the Ten Commandments and of the New Testament reaffirmation of the law of love. The Bible indeed does not spell out in precise detail what in every instance is right and what in every circumstance is an act of love. Man is an ethical being called to make moral decisions within the concrete situations of life. But the Bible provides man with a moral framework. It is this moral framework that is the point of reference for every ethical decision in the concrete situations of life, a reference by which man is able to make a judgment as to what in specific situations is right or wrong. Without such a point of permanent moral reference, man's attempt to judge what is good is a ship at sea without direction.

It is precisely such a frame of reference that is lacking in Bishop John A. T. Robinson's plea for a "new morality" in his new book *Christian Morals Today*.* In this little book, written after his well-publicized *Honest to God,* the Bishop of Woolwich urges that all Christian morality moves between two poles, which may be variously described as fixity and freedom, law and love, and authority and experience. The "old morality" no less than the "new morality" moves between these poles, the only difference being the direction of the movement. The "old morality," says Robinson, moves from fixity toward freedom, from law toward love, from authority toward

* Westminster Press, 1964.

experience. The "new morality," for which he pleads, moves from freedom to fixity, from love toward law, and from experience toward authority. It may be said here, and shown later, that Robinson's "new morality" never actually moves from a free experience of love to a fixed law that has binding authority. He in fact begins with the binding principle of Christian *agape* and never arrives at any moral law whose fulfillment is necessarily good and whose infraction is necessarily immoral.

But first let us trace his thought. Robinson contends that the "old morality" locates the unchanging element of Christian ethics "in the *content* of the commands" (p. 11). And he continues to describe the "old morality" by adding, "There are certain things which are always right and others which are always wrong. These absolute Christian standards are eternally valid, and remain unchanging in the midst of relativity and flux" (p. 11). Adherents of this morality assert, says Robinson, that the task of the Church is to proclaim these standards and to summon people of any time and age to apply them and live by them.

In the "new morality" the constant element in Christian ethics is not located in all or any of the specific commandments, but in "sacrificial, unselfregarding *agape*" (p. 12). The ethical task of the Christian is not in the keeping of these commandments, but in the exercise of freedom to decide in the light of love (*agape*) what is right and what is wrong at any given point in the ever-changing human situation. Robinson writes, "In Christian ethics the only pure commandment is the command to love." The various commandments of Jesus and of Paul "are comprehended under the one command of love and based upon it." And he immediately adds, "Apart from this there are no unbreakable rules" (p. 16).

To illustrate that there are, other than the demand of *agape,* no unbreakable moral rules, Robinson repeatedly points to the fact that what the Church has allowed in one age it has condemned in another. One may, indeed one must, admit this. Yet this empirical fact does not prove Robinson's thesis that no moral law is always binding, unless one regards the Church as infallible in its moral teaching. In this connection Robinson also points to the matter of war. He appears to concede that a conventional war could be a just war, but he regards a nuclear war as excluding the possibility of a just war. But does this prove his thesis that no moral law, in this case a moral law relative to war, is always binding? If the nature of warfare has so radically changed in the nuclear age that a just war is no longer a possibility, then it is not the morality contained in the law which permitted the just war that has changed. It is rather the nature of warfare that has so radically changed that the moral precept of a just war is no longer relevant. It is not morality, then, but warfare that has changed. If, for example, the defenses against nuclear warfare can be developed to the point where nuclear warfare no longer means something like total destruction, then the force of the morality of the just war will again be relevant even in the nuclear age.

One might also ask Robinson what his "new morality," which recognizes no ethical constant except "sacrificial, unselfregarding *agape,*" can possibly have to say about a "just" war. A Christian ethic that recognizes only the demands of *agape,* defined as "sacrificial, unselfregarding" love, excludes justice and denies it a rightful place in Christian ethics.

77

Here, then, lies the distinctive feature of Robinson's "new morality": Love is the only constant moral imperative; and this means in Robinson's thought that no commandment of the Bible, neither the Ten Commandments nor any of the New Testament, has the force of a permanent standard of reference for moral conduct. Robinson indeed believes that every biblical commandment is an expression of *agape,* but he contends that none embodies the demand of *agape* in such form and content that it is permanently binding. Each is only a paradigm of the one pure commandment of *agape.* None is *per se* binding on us, nor for that matter binding on anyone. Robinson, for example, refers to the biblical injunctions about male and female, husband and wife, and those other codes that govern personal connections "in the Lord." He asserts that they are only "human constructions," and he presses the point that it is essential that we recognize them as such (p. 18).

Further light is thrown on Robinson's "new morality" when we observe that he refers, with agreement, to the position of C. F. D. Moule that "the ten commandments are not the basis of Christian morals, on which an ethic of loves goes on to build" (p. 23). Whatever Moule means by this, what it means to Robinson is clear. Again, Robinson asserts that it is "dangerous" for us "to regard the teaching of Jesus itself as a code, to see it as laying down for all Christians at all times, or indeed for any Christians at any time, what they should do" (p. 23). Here Robinson is not merely saying that changing circumstances call different moral demands into play. He is asserting that no moral law is binding; even the moral laws Jesus laid down were not binding on the people of his time to whom they were addressed (p. 26). Consequently a determination of the moral standards that ought to have governance over our lives cannot be made by an appeal to " 'the Bible' " (p. 31). Love alone, and only love, is the binding moral imperative upon all men.

How then do men of the "new morality" determine what is morally right and wrong? Not by reference to biblical injunctions. On the contrary, the Word of God, says Robinson, is present in every moral situation, "yet not as proposition but as presence" (p. 38). No biblical moral precepts can tell us what to do in a concrete moral situation. Guidance will come if the Christian gives himself in love and trusts God; he will then find God or, what for Robinson is the same thing, discover the demands of *agape* for the concrete situation. If he heeds the demand, he will find himself ministering to Christ. "This trust," admits Robinson, "is not the clear-cut confidence of a deductive ethic. Inevitably it appears less authoritative than that of 'the old morality.' But for some of us it may be the only assurance we have, and I am not convinced the New Testament necessarily promises more" (p. 39).

Corresponding to his rejection of the binding moral quality of biblical commandments is Robinson's assertion that "there is not a whole list of things which are 'sins' *per se*" (p. 16). Honest with his convictions and his readers, and consistent with the character of his "new morality," Robinson frankly asserts that while stealing, lying, killing, adultery are usually destructive of human relationships and therefore wrong, they are not necessarily and always wrong. They cannot be cited as a list of sins. They are only sinful if and when they are in violation of the one and only pure demand, the demand of *agape*. In certain circumstances any or all of these actions can be an expression of *agape*. When they are, they are morally acceptable. Here Robinson's ethics are that of the play *Tea and Sympathy*.*

There are at least two moral rules that give Robinson some difficulty. They are rape and cruelty to children. He admits that it is "so inconceivable" that rape and cruelty to children could ever be an expression of *agape* that "one might say without much fear of contradiction that they are for Christians always wrong" (p. 16). Yet he cannot say that they are, *without any fear of contradiction,* always wrong. To do so would mean that Robinson has a list of at least two things that are always *per se* sinful — and the inherent character of his "new morality" excludes even a brief list of things that are *per se* sinful. Moreover, it is basic to his ethic that no moral law but only *agape* contains (or is) the one permanent ethical constant. If rape were always wrong, then the content of *this* law would be as constant as that of *agape,* and to accept this would be to fall back into the "old morality." For the "old morality" in distinction from the "new morality" finds "the unchanging element in Christian ethics in the *content* of the commands" (p. 11).

Because there are no specific commandments whose reflections of *agape* always and everywhere require the form of conduct specified in the form of the commandment, there are no *settled* "limits of pre-marital sex for engaged couples" (p. 32). The only permanently binding precept here is that conduct in this relationship express *agape* for the other person. One cannot, says Robinson, decide these limits by an appeal to the law, " 'Fornication is always wrong' " (p. 33).

---

* In defending D. H. Lawrence's book *Lady Chatterley's Lover,* Robinson describes an adulterous relationship of Lady Chatterley as "a kind of holy communion."

Robinson views homosexuality from the same perspective. He admits that homosexuality, like many other forms of human conduct, is *usually* sinful. But he contends that it is not always and *per se* sinful. This, too, cannot go on a list of things that are always wrong. Robinson comments on the Wolfenden Report, which asserts that "homosexual behavior between consenting adults in private should no longer be a criminal offence." Robinson agrees with this, for how could he properly regard it as a criminal offense if it is not necessarily a moral offense?* "We have come to a much greater awareness of the facts," he says, "particularly about the causes of homosexuality and about the truly appalling social consequences of our present law for blackmail, for suicide, and [significantly] for the denial to a sizable minority of our population of any deep, free or secure personal relationships" (pp. 40, 41). If homosexuality, according to Robinson, is engaged in out of a sense of *agape* for the other person, it is not morally wrong but rather productive of a deep, free, secure personal relationship.

WHAT THEN DOES ROBINSON MEAN WHEN HE SAYS that the "new morality" moves from freedom toward fixity, love toward law, and from experience toward authority, whereas the "old morality" moves in the reverse direction? He means that *agape* comes to expression in moral laws and precepts. He asserts that the Church and the State and society, including young people, need these laws. These laws serve "catechetical and disciplinary purposes." But none are unconditionally

---

* One can, of course, hold that it is a moral offense without holding that it should also be a criminal offense.

binding. They do not necessarily show what is right and good in every instance, and the breaking of them is not necessarily and always wrong. None are timeless, and none necessarily and everywhere obligatory. They may be questioned, and today, says Robinson, they are being questioned by many people. Now that the old moral codes and regulations are being questioned, it is the duty of the Christian, of the Church, to admit that they are questionable and to make fresh determinations in the light of *agape* as to what is today right and wrong. He hopes that the State will also do as much. To quote him: "But my point is that when these are questioned, as they are being questioned, the Christian is driven back to base them not on law ('Fornication is always wrong') but on love, on what a deep concern for persons as whole persons, in their entire social context, really requires" (p. 33).

Bishop Robinson quotes an article by James Hemming that appeared in the *New Society* (September, 1963) under the title "Moral Education in Chaos": "One element of the moral change of the recent era is that the morality of obedience to external absolutes is being replaced by the morality of involvement and discovery." Robinson asks, "What are we to make as Christians of this frank plea for a morality of involvement and discovery?" And his answer is: "I believe we should welcome it" (p. 37). He continues, "Indeed, I would go further and accept what he [Hemming] says later: 'Both scientific and religious viewpoints are, today, humanisms. But neither is only a humanism because each accepts that existence itself is shrouded in mystery. Each may wish to put something different into that mystery. One group may put a personal God there; the other a question mark; but each will agree that the ground of man's being is humanism within a mystery. This is the new starting-point. It provides a vast unifying common ground in terms of human involvement and purpose." To this the Bishop says, "I agree with him — not necessarily with where he ends (I do not know whether he would call himself a Christian), but with where he begins" (pp. 37, 38). And Robinson warns the Christian that as he searches together with the modern man for the good, he must not give "the slightest suggestion of intellectual or moral slumming. Christians cannot say, 'Yes, we will join you in your search — but, of course, though you do not know it, we know in advance that certain things are always wrong.' If they think they know this, then they had much better wait for the others at the end of the road" (p. 38).

With this, the weakest and most dangerous part of Robinson's "new morality" lies exposed. Nothing is sinful in itself. No moral law is unconditionally binding. Each individual is left, in the involvement of love for his neighbor, to discover for himself, in the light of the demands of *agape,* whether any conceivable human action is morally right or morally wrong. The knowledge of right and wrong is not given in the biblical precepts, nor in the codes of Church or State. All these may be questioned. The Christian has no guarantee in any instance that he will come to the knowledge of good and evil. He can only trust God — and God is not only on the rocks, as the adherents of the "old morality" think, God is also in the rapids. In the rapids of life the individual, acting out of *agape,* must discover the answer to the question, "What doth the Lord require of thee, O man?"

83

SUCH A VIEW OF ETHICS HAS ONLY UNESSENTIAL CON-
nections with a biblically grounded Christian ethic.
Bishop Robinson provides his own best commentary on
the "new morality" for which he pleads when he says,
"Any ethic which is genuinely Christian will always be
open to the charge of destroying the law. . . . Anti-
nomianism is always a false accusation, but I would immediately suspect there was something sub-Christian
about an ethic which did not provoke it" (p. 22).

Whatever else Robinson's "new morality" provokes, it
surely provokes the question of the competency of a
man, even if he be a bishop, to construct a Christian
ethic if he admits that he can never be completely confi-
dent that an act of murder or rape is always morally
wrong. Anyone who would sketch a new morality and
plead publicly for it should wait until such time as he
can cope with such matters as rape and cruelty to children, for something is essentially wrong with a morality
that cannot get these into the categories of immorality.
Nor is this "new morality" able to meet the required
moral response to the conduct of an Adolf Eichmann,
or to that of the organizational man who takes his ethics
from the company. A morality that leaves it to the
individual to discover whether any conceivable human
action is right or wrong cannot mend the seams of the
garment of twentieth-century morals.